Table of Contents

Introduction

Chapter 1: Getting started: Things you will need and need to know inorder to get started

Chapter 2: Crochet Basics: Hook handling and chain making

Chapter 3: Stitches be plentiful: An arsenal of different crochet stitches that every beginner should know

Chapter 4: Decorative stitches and patterns: How to add a dash of pretty with crotchet

Chapter 5: Crochet abbreviations and phrases decoded

Conclusion

Bonus Chapter: Knitting for Beginners

Introduction

I want to thank you and congratulate you for downloading the book, "Crocheting – 7 Simple Steps to Learning How to Crochet and Create Easy to Make Crochet Stitches and Crochet Patterns Today!"

This book will gift upon you the tools and knowledge that every novice should be aware of when they first begin their crocheting adventure.

When you first decide to crochet, it can be quite a tough and confusing time. You will come across a lot of strange conceptions, phrases and equipment that will make you furrow your eyebrows in confusion. This book is meant to decode this new and alien world so you can begin your journey of being an able and skilled individual at crocheting. You could become like those people on Youtube videos who make it seem easy and effortless with their yarn and needle moving at an astounding speed. However, when you first start off you may end up with tangled yarn, strange looking stitches and an inner feeling of utter hopelessness.

But don't lose hope. The important thing to remember, like with all things in life, is that practice makes perfect. This book will give you the basic tools of the trade, the knowledge of how to use the equipment, the simple stitches you can employ and the jargon you will run across. Gaining an understanding of this, the components or ingredients of the craft, will set you up for success. You won't exactly be jumping into making marvelous hats and delicate roses. You will begin with the basics, which are in this book, and then move onto being a super talented pro crocheting like a master; you will have a black belt for crocheting.

In this book, we will thoroughly go over the basic building blocks of the craft, arming you to the teeth for your crocheting adventure. The first chapter will introduce you to the tools of the trade. What you will be working with when you start crocheting so you won't wander aimlessly in the craft store surrounded by strange merchandise. You will know what you need and you will also know what each item actually does. Once you know the tools of the trade and properly more about yarn then you ever actually wanted to know, it is time to start to learn how to actually use the tools. So we will give you the essential information on how to begin to crochet. We will look at all the basics, for example, how to a slip knot, how to make a chain and the various types of major stitch that you will need to learn. In Chapter 3, we will let our love of everything pretty shine through and will show you how to create some different ascetically pleasing stitches that are fun to try out.

The last chapter will help you decode some of the crochet jargon that you may run across while crocheting. Because let me tell you, when you first come across a crochet pattern it can be a bewildering experience with a sea of strange letters and numbers. It will feel like trying to read Latin when the only Latin phrase you know is carpe diem. In other words, it will be really really difficult. This book is your starting platform to your crocheting odyssey. It will not show you how to create amazing and awe inspiring creations, rather it will gift you with the tools so you can in the future be capable of creating amazing things.

Thanks again for downloading this book and I hope you enjoy it!

Chapter 1: Getting started: Things you will need and need to know in order to get started

To be seen as a competent crocheter, you will need to gather four pieces of key equipment. These will be extremely easy to find and inexpensive to obtain from any local craft store. In this chapter, we have listed the required items and also a little bit of information on each.

What you will need?

To begin to crochet, you will need four chief items. These being yarn, a crochet hook, a darning needle and a pair of scissors.

Yarn: Yarn is quite an ambiguous term as there is a myriad of different variations available, which you will become aware of as soon as you enter a craft store. Therefore, there are a few specific characteristics of your yarn that you should look for in order to find the right material for your crocheting. Below we have presented a few yarn do's.

Do go wild when deciding upon the color of your wool. Do not limit yourself to a few safe muted colors but pick a few bold and eye-catching colors as well. Also, Light colors may be better for beginners as it will be easier to see the stitches. Lastly, let your personality shine through with your colors. If you are a rather reserved person, then you may wish to stick with monochrome colors, shades such as grays, crèmes, and browns. Where on the other hand if you are often described as the life of the party, you may lean more towards colors which are bold and dynamic, these could be yellows, reds, and purples. Crafting is a great way to express yourself and let others know who you are.

Do decide upon a smooth textured yarn rather than a thick textured one. For a beginner, it can be quite difficult to work with the latter. When you become more competent in the craft, you can venture out and try different textures of yarn but for now stick with a nice smooth type.

Do try wool if possible. Wool yarn is a great material to start off with as it is easy to use and if you make a mistake, wool is easy to unravel. Wool is also a pleasant material to have your socks or a scarf made from as it is pleasant to touch.

Do pick an appropriate yarn weight according to your specific needs. The yarn weight will be displayed on the label in a single bold number ranging from 1-6. For crocheting, you should use a yarn with a weight of 4 or higher. So remember to look at the label so you are aware of your yarn weight. **Do** get plenty of yarn. There is nothing worse than to be interrupted while happily crocheting because you have ran out of yarn. So make sure you stock up on yarn, as too much yarn is better than not enough.

Do decide upon a nice simple type of yarn. Do not get those flashy types that resemble a giant fur ball or have appealing sparkles. These ascetically pleasing types of yarn may look great but they are really frustrating to work with if you are a novice.

A crochet hook: This will be your tool that you will wield when you partake in crocheting. When viewed, it resembles a strange thin stick with a hooked top. It is quite simple in appearance but when brandished correctly it can create a whole host of impressive items.

Crochet hooks come in various sizes and are also made from different types of material. The size parameters range from 2-16mm. The sizing system in the US is based on a letter scheme. It starts at the smallest that is labeled as a B, which is 2.25mm in size, all the way to the largest size known as Q, which is 16mm. The size that you decide upon will determine the type of yarn that can be used. This is as follows: the smaller the hook, the finer the yarn and the larger the hook, the thicker the yarn.

Also, a crochet hook can be made from various different types of material, including steel, plastic, wood, aluminum and wood. The type you decide upon will be largely down to personal preference, depending on what feels the best and what you can work with the best. For example, you may prefer the rough feel of wood over the slippery feel of steel.

There is also a slight difference in shape with the hooks depending on whether or not you decide to go with an inlined hook and one that was not in line. The difference lies in the shape or protruding of the hook. With the inlined hook, the curve of the top is in line with the rest of the hook which is contrasted with the hook that is not in line, which has an extended curving hook. The hook that is not inline has a more tapered shape whereas the inlined hook is straighter down.

A darning needle: This is used to sew the edges of your crocheted creations so that they are neat and uniform and not messy looking. A darning needle can be easily found in a craft or art store or properly around your grandmother's house.

A pair of scissors: A simple pair of scissors that you will use to cut yarn.

Chapter 2: Crochet Basics: Hook handling and chain making

Grab your needle and yarn; it's time to crochet.

As a novice crocheter, it can be quite daunting when you first gaze upon your hook and yarn. It can end up being quite an accomplishment when you first start out, not to get the yarn tangled into a chaotic mess or stab yourself with the hook. It will all be quite alien to you. But you can calm yourself because this foreignness and strangeness will soon fade into comfortable and skilled familiarity. The hook will become an extension of yourself and the wool will be worked by your hands quickly and skillfully.

How to properly handle your crochet hook

The very first thing you will need to learn before you actually start to crochet is how to handle your hook. There are two chief ways to hold your crochet hook and how you decide to do so is largely up to personal preference.

1. The first way will look like you are holding a dinner knife. Your thumb and middle finger will rest on the grip, your index finger will rest on the side of the hook and the end of the hook will be pressing touching your palm.

2. The second way will look like you are holding a pencil or pen. Pick up your hook and hold it how you would naturally hold a pencil. Don't overall think about this, just pick it up and naturally move to that hand position. Your thumb and index finger should be pressed on the grip on opposite sides of the hook and the middle finger should be resting near the top of the hook. The end of the hook should be elevated.

These are the chief manners of holding a crochet hook. Try both ways and decide upon the one that feels most natural. There is no right or wrong here. It is what feels most natural and comfortable for you.

How to make a foundation crochet chain

Most crocheted creations begin with a foundation chain. In patterns, this will be described as ch. To start this chain, you will need to get your yarn onto your hook. This is done with a slip knot. The way that people perform a slip knot can vary depending on how they were taught. Methods learned in childhood can stay with a person their entire lives [this is also evident with the bunny ear method when tying shoe laces]. Here we will show you one way to create a slip knot but if you have your own quirky way then you should stick with it. I came across someone who pretended their slipknot was a pretzel and was able to work with it using this imagery.

How to make a slip note

1. Grab your yarn and hook. Taking your yarn, unravel it so you have around 6inches of free yarn. This yarn will have the free end and the attached end, the end that runs to the ball of yarn. You will need to remember these two terms through the instructions, the free end, and the attached end. Taking the piece of yarn, make a small loop. The free end should on top. Place the hook in the loop. To do this, insert it over the top of the loop and under the other piece of the loop until you hook it over the free end. Pull this yarn so you bring this loop onto your crochet hook. Pull the ends of the yarn, so it is secure on your hook. However, don't pull too hard you don't want it to be too tight. There will need to be a little mobility with the knot or it will be too difficult to work with.

How to make your foundation chain

Now that you have attached your yarn to your hook, you can start to actually crochet. Here we will show you how to do a basic crochet stitch and make your foundation chain.

1. First you need to pick up your yarn. There is a specific way that you will need to hold it in order to crochet effortlessly. Wrap your yarn around your pinkie finger so that the free end ends up facing upwards towards the rest of your fingers. Take the yarn and bring it to your index finger, wrapping it partially around it. It should be lightly resting over the index finger, not tightly wrapped around it. The fingers that are holding the yarn, your pinkie, and index fingers, should be slightly curved towards your palm so the yarn does not fall.

2. The hand not holding the yarn should be holding the hook. Place your thumb and middle finger just below your slipknot.

3. Wrap the yarn around the hook. This should be done from the front to back, so coming in from the back wrap the yarn over until it is resting in the curve of the top of the hook.

4. Using your crochet hook, pull on the hooked yarn until you have drawn it through the slip knot. You have successfully made your first chain stitch. Continue until you have the amount of ch stitches that you wish for or are required for the specific pattern that you are working with.

How to count crochet stitches?

This is an important thing to learn as certain crochet projects require a very specific amount of stitches. To do this, count how many V shapes you have along your chain. However, it is important to note that the your starting slip knot does not count as a stitch nor does the loop connected to the hook. These are the individual stitches.

Chapter 3: Stitches be plentiful: An arsenal of different crochet stitches that every beginner should know.

There is an array of different types of crochet stitches out there, each fashioning a different look for your crotched creations. However, because you are only just starting out it is best not to get overwhelmed with the many varieties and stick with a few simple types that are relatively easy to learn. In this chapter, we will look at the single crochet stitch, double stitch, triple stitch and a half double stitch.

The single crotchet stitch

The single stitch, abbreviated as **sc** in patterns, is great for beginners as it is one of the easiest stitches to master.

How to:

1. Grab your hook with your chain stitch and your yarn

2. Insert your hook into your chain. The easiest way to do this is by pushing it through the "V" shape that you should see on your foundation chain. There are other ways to insert your hook, but this is a nice simple way for a beginner as the V shape is easy to identify.

3. Once you have pushed the crotchet hook through the center of the V, wrap your yarn around the hook and catch it using the curved top. These methods of wrapping the yarn around the hook are referred to as yarn over or hook the yarn. So if you come across these terms in a pattern or a series of instructions that is what it refers to.

4. Using the curved top, pull the yarn through the V or the single stitch of the chain. After you have done this you should have two separate loops of wool on your hook.

5. Once again wrap your wool around the top of your hook, going from back to the front until it is resting in the curve of the hook. Pull this wool through the two loops on your hook.

6. After doing this, you should still have a single loop on your hook. Well done, you have successfully done a single crochet stitch. Keep on going until you have done the whole chain but

do not stitch the slip knot.

7. **Once you have completed the first row, it is time to begin the second. First, you will need to move or turn your crochet 180 degrees so it is facing the opposite direction. Do this in a counter clockwise direction.**

8. **The way you crotchet the second row and each corresponding row will vary from the previously stated instructions. First, rather than sticking the hook through the V shape, you will push it through the last stitch that you did on the previous row. You can do this by pushing through the center of it, under the dual loops of yarn at the top border of your crochet creation.**

9. **After you have pushed your hook through, hook the yarn and pull it through the stitch. You should now have two loops of yarn on your hook. Once more hook the yarn and pull it through both loops on your hook.**

10. **When you get to the end of your row, you will want to chain one stitch, meaning you wrap your yarn around your hook one time and pull it through the stitch.**

Note: Because this is a single crochet stitch you may notice that your work curls up a bit. This is nothing to worry about.

The double crotchet stitch

The double crotchet stitch is another type of stitch that you should become familiar with as it is commonly used in patterns. It is abbreviated as **dc**.

How to:

1. The first thing you need to do is actually done while working your chain. When you are making your chain, make sure you add three more stitches loops of yarn on your hook.

2. Once you reach the end of the row, you are going to chain three stitches using the method we discussed in the previous chapter. When double crocheting, it is important that you remember to always chain three stitches to get to your next row.

3. Next turn your work around. You then want to push your hook through the second stitch, under the dual loops of yarn, and

continue crocheting in the method we just discussed.

4. Note: The main difference between a single then you actually need for your pattern or work. This is because you will be starting from the fourth stitch of your chain this time rather than the second.

5. Begin you push your hook through the stitch; you need to wrap the yarn around the hook from back to front so the yarn is resting in the crook of the hook.

6. Hold the yarn so it doesn't slip off and push the hook through the fourth stitch on your chain.

7. Once you have pushed your hook through the stitch, wrap your yarn again and pull it through it back through your chain stitch. You should now have three loops or stitches on your hook.

8. Again wrap your yarn around the hook, back to front, and pull it back through two loops of yarn on your hook.

Once again, and I know this may be getting a tad repetitive but stick with me, but wrap your yarn again around your hook and pull it through the last two remaining and double crochet stitch, is that with the latter your wrap your yarn first before pushing through the chain stitch.

The half double stitch

The half double stitch is kind of the middle ground between a single stitch and a double where methods from both stitches are combined.

How to:

1. First, make your chain.

2. Next, you are going to begin in the same manner of a second crochet stitch where you loop the wool before pushing through the stitch.

3. Once you have hooked the yarn, you will push the hook through the third chain stitch. Yarn over again and pull it through the stitch.

4. Yarn over again and then pull it through all three loops or stitches that are on your hook. And you have successfully completed your first half double stitch.

5. When you reach the end of your row and are getting ready to turn, you chain on two additional stitches.

6. Turn your work around. Wrap your yarn and then push your hook into the second stitch, not the first. You will push your hook through the middle of the stitch, below the loops of yarn.

The triple crochet stitch

Sometimes referred to as a treble stitch, this variation of crochet stitch will create a fabric that is quite loose.

How to:

1. Start off with your chain. Wrap your yarn twice around your hook and then push through the fifth chain stitch.

2. Wrap the yarn again, back to front, and pull it back through the stitch.

3. Wrap the yarn once again and pull it through the first two stitches on your hook. Hook the yarn one last time and pull it through the two remaining loops of yarn on the hook. Continue on until you have finished the row.

4. Turn your work over and chain four chain stitches. Then wrap the yarn twice around the hook and push it through the second stitch, not the first. Continue as we have already instructed.

The Slip Stitch

The slip stitch is the smallest of the crochet stitches, but it is hardly ever used in the same manner as the other stitches, meaning it is not used to create entire creations. Rather it is occasionally used as a feature of some works, for example with seams, edging or shaping your work.

How to:

1. To begin, make your slip knot and chain.

2. Next, insert your hook into the first stitch of your row that you have just finished making. This row can be made from any type of stitch.

3. Yarn over and pull the yarn through the stitch.

4. At this stage, you should have two loops of yarn on your hook. Now, we will want to pull the hook all the way through both loops of yarn. After you have done this you should still have one stitch

left on your hook.

5. When you reach the end of the row, instead of chaining more stitches on, you simply turn your work around and start immediately slip stitching into the next row.

Chapter 4: Decorative stitches and patterns: How to add a dash of pretty with crotchet

Armed with your hook and yarn, you can actively transform basic and monotonous items into beautiful and intricate pieces of art. If a sea of monotonous green or brown does not appeal to you, you could instead create crochet creations that have fantastic and quirky patterns. In this chapter, we will look at methods that you can use in order to give your work a little more oomph and appeal.

The Moss or Granite stitch

The moss or granite stitch is a great stitch for beginners and it incorporates a different and appealing appearance to your next crochet creation.

How to:

1.Start off by making a foundation chain that has twenty stitches using the method we have discussed in a previous chapter.

2.Next, slip stitch into the third chain stitch from the hook. If you have forgotten how to slip stitch simply go back to the previous chapter.

3. With the next stitch on the row, you will want to do a half double crochet stitch.

4.You will then repeat step 2 and 3 for the remainder of the chain stitch. So, for odd stitches, 5, 7, 9 etc., you would do the slip stitch and with the even stitches you would do the half double crochet stitch variant.

5. At the end of the chain, you will chain on one chain stitch and then turn your work.

6.For the next row, you will do the opposite of what you did previously. So on your row where there is a slip stitch you will want to contrast it with a half double crochet and where you have done a half double crochet in the previous row you will do a slip stitch.

7.In regards to this series of instructions, you should have finished the last row with a half double crochet so for the first stitch of the next row you should begin with a slip stitch.

Note: You should be able to easily distinguish between the two types of stitches based on size alone. The slip stitch will be a lot smaller than the half double.

The Crunch stitch

1.To begin this kind of stitch, create a foundation chain. The number you chain on should be a multiple of 2 +1.

2.Row one: Skip the first 2 chain stitches, do a slip stitch in the third chain stitch. After this, do a half double crochet in the next chain stitch followed by another slip stitch into the next chain stitch. Repeat this series of stitches until you reach the end of the row. Turn your work.

3. Row Two: First you need to chain two. On your row, find the half double crochet stitch. You should be able to see it quite clearly, as it will be larger than the slip stitch. Into this half double stitch, work a slip stitch. Follow this up by doing a half double crochet into the next stitch of the row, which should be a slip stitch. The next stitch should be a slip stitch that you work into the next stitch of the row. Continue this sequence until you reach the end of the row. At the turning chain, work in slip stitch.

4. You should then repeat the steps involved in row two until you have reached you're sought after size.

The Primrose stitch

You may be a Hunger Games fan and consequently love anything to do with it even if it is simply matching names of a character and stitch. Or you may simply want to stay classy; if so this stitch may be right down your alley. This is an elegant stitch that is suitable for beginner levels.

How to:

1. Make a slipknot and complete your foundation chain. This chain should have multiples of 3 +2.

2.Once the chain has been made, do a single crotchet into your third chain stitch from your hook. After you have done that, you need to chain two stitches using the chain method. Next, do another single crotchet again into the third chain stitch.

3.Skip the next two stitches on the chain and then repeat the process we have only just previously done. So, do 1 sc, ch 2 and then 1sc. After you have finished the sequence you once again simply skip two stitches and do the same series of stitches as before, 1 sc, ch 2 and the 1sc. Do this until you have reached the final stitch on the row.

4.With the last stitch on the row, you need to do a half double crotchet stitch.

Turn the work around and you can now start row 1.

5. Row one: You will begin by chaining three. Look at your row, you should have a series of peaks or elevated portions. In these parts, you will do three double crotchet stitches. Continue until you have reached the end of the row.

6.In the end there should be a part sticking out, this is called a turning chain. Into this, you will do a double crotchet stitch. Turn your work around and we will start row two.

7.Row two: Begin by chaining two. Once you have done this, work a single stitch [1 sc] into the third stitch on the row so skip the first two of the row. Then chain two [ch 2] and then work a single crochet back into the same stitch, the third stitch of the row. Repeat this sequence until you have reached the turning chain. Into the turning chain, you will do a half double stitch.

8.Now that you know how to carry out row 1 and 2, you will repeat each of them until you reach your desirable length and shape.

The Triangle Stitch

1.First create the chain. The number of chain stitches you make should be in multiples of three plus one.

2.Prep row: Before you get down to business, we will need to do a prep row. For this, you will do a single crochet into the second chain stitch. You will continue to do this for the entire row, so a single crochet stitches every second chain stitch. When you have finished the row, turn your work.

3.Row one: To start this row off, you will need to chain four. Skip the first stitch on the row, yarn over and then pick up the loop of yarn in the next stitch. Continue doing this moving down the row, so yarn over and pick up the stitch loop, yarn over and pick up the stitch. You need to do this a grand total of three times. In the end, you should have seven separate loops of yarn on your hook. Yarn over one more time and then pull your hook through all seven loops of yarn. This is your first triangle.

4.Now chain two and then yarn over and then pick up the same first stitch used in your previous triangle. Repeat three times the process of yarning over and picking up the next stitch. At the end of this stage, you should once again have seven loops of yarn on your hook. Pull back with your hook all the way through all seven loops of yarn.

5.Repeat these actions until you come to the end of the row. At the end of the row in order to finish up, you will need to do a single chain and then a half double chain into the turning chain. Turn your work so you can start row two.

6.Row two: To kick things off with this row, chain a single stitch. Next do a single crochet into the first stitch of your row. Work another single crochet into the first chain one space [this is described in the next chapter].

7.Next do two single crochet stitches in each individual chain two space. Repeat this step until you have reached the end of the row. To finish the row, you need to do a single crochet into the second chain stitch of the turning chain. Turn your work and repeat row one and two instructions until you have reached the shape you desire.

The Star Stitch

1.To begin this stitch, you need to make your foundation chain. The number of stitches in this chain should be in multiples of two plus one.

2.Row one: To begin, push your hook through the second chain stitch and pull up a loop. You do this by pushing your hook through the stitch, pulling the yarn over and then pull it through. Do the same thing for the next four chain stitches. At the end of this, you should have six loops on your hook.

3.Next yarn over and pull your hook through all six loops of yarn. Now chain one, this is going to act as the eye of the star.

4.Next you need to insert your hook into this "eye" of the star, the chain stitch that you just made and draw it through. For the next star, you will basically do the same thing you did with the previous one. So starting from the point where your last star finished, draw your hook through the loop of yarn and do the same thing for the next two stitches. You should end up with six loops of yarn on your hook.

5.Now yarn over and draw through all the loops of yarn on your hook. Yarn over and close the star by doing a chain stitch. Repeat this series of steps from the symbol inserted into these instructions.

6.Once you have reached the last stitch of the row, make your star as usual but afterward you will need to work in a half double stitch. Turn your work and then it is time to start row two.

7.Row two: We will start things off by chaining one. Next, we will work a single crochet into the half double crochet that we just did on the previous row.

8.Next we do a single crochet stitch into the eye of the star. Following this we work in two single crochet stitches into every star center until the end of the row.

9.At the end of the row, we will do a single crochet stitch into the top of the turning chain. Turn over your work.

10. Chain three and then repeat the steps on how to make each individual star until you have reached the desired length for your creation.

Chapter 5: Crochet abbreviations and phrases decoded

Ch: If you see this in a pattern, it stands for a chain stitch.

Dc: If you see this in a pattern, it means a double crochet stitch.

Hdc: if you see this in a pattern, it means a half double crochet stitch.

Pull up a loop: This means to pull or grab the yarn with the curved top end of your hook. This is normally done to make a loop of yarn that is pulled onto your hook.

Sc: When you see this on a pattern, it means single crochet stitch.

Slst: If you see this in a pattern, it means a slip stitch.

Tr: If you see this in a pattern, it means a triple stitch.

Turning chain:Is the chain of stitches that are made when you add chain stitches at the end of a row.

Turn over: This means to turn your work around when you have finished the row.

Work into a chain space: This is where instead of working into a particular stitch, you rather work into the gap or bridge made by two chains.

Yarn over: This means to wrap your yarn around your hook from back to front so it ends up resting in the top of your hook.

Yo: If you see this in a pattern, it means yarn over.

Conclusion

Thank you again for downloading this book!

The next step is to go out and actually start making crocheted creations. There are so many different things you can create with your hands, a hook, yarn and the knowledge that you have gained from this book.

Finally, if you enjoyed this book, then I'd like to ask you for a favor, would you be kind enough to leave a review for this book on Amazon? It'd be greatly appreciated!

Click here to leave a review for this book on Amazon!

Thank you and good luck!

Bonus Chapter: Knitting for Beginners

Nurturing a hobby like knitting may sound outdated for today's world, when everyone is rushing to reach their goals and destinations. No one has time to leisurely sit and visit with those near and dear to them; why do we need to do that when we can simply pick up our cell phone. Whether it's about keeping in contact or presenting gifts to them, everything is at our fingertips. With the click of a button the work is done, but do you really think that's enough? I know, those branded shops are also there to fulfill your wishes, but will you ever forget that blue sweater that your mother knit for your first day of school? You won't because that was not bought from the shop, but knit just for you with lots of love.

Nothing can replace the charm of those pink gloves, knit by your grandmother for your sixth birthday, or the scarf that has been knit by the lovely wife for her beloved husband. No matter how expensive those gifts bought from the shop may be, they will never compare to the gifts that represent our dear one's love and care for us.

Knitting has its own appeal, which many who are already in love and savvy with this hobby have already discovered. You may have already become famous in your group of friends or among your kith and kin for your outstanding knitting talent. Each time your new knit and stylish scarves, gloves or shrugs make others jealous, those envious facial expressions undoubtedly encourage you to hone your talent. Our attempt with this book is to help those who, though they are already in love with knitting, don't know from where to begin this hobby. Although a multitude of information can be found all over the internet, finding a neat and hazard free way to start always seems difficult for beginners. Keeping that in mind, this book has been designed to provide maximum benefits to the beginner; especially those who are completely new to the term "knitting". I believe, at the end of the journey, you will find that knitting is not as difficult as it seems to be.

Unlike other hobbies such as gardening or reading, knitting is less time consuming and even helps to enhance multitasking capability. Moreover, according to medical science, it also has some undeniable health benefits. Along with maintaining strong and excellent hand- brain coordination, it has been proven beneficial for mental health too. Usually, those who are indulging in knitting rarely find themselves suffering from a bad mood or depression and eventually find themselves happier compared to others. Knitting plays an important role in keeping our brain active. While you are struggling with those complicated stitches or trying to secure dropped stitches, you are actually helping your brain to work more which enhances its working capabilities. This beautiful skill allows room for experimenting with different types of stitches, which means there will never be a shortage of creative ideas and projects. There is no doubt that you are on the right track if you choose knitting as your favorite hobby to be passionate about.

For elderly people, knitting is a wonderful pastime, especially when they have no one to give them company and they are retired and unable to get out of the house much. Experimenting with those complicated stitches does not allow them time for feeling lonely. If they are beginners, joining a knitting class can be a great help for them, they can make friends along with learning knitting. Younger generations are also on the list of admirers, particularly when they want to show off their talents. Knitting as a hobby not only allows their talents to flourish, but keeps them away from any wrongdoings by giving them something meaningful to take up their time. They remain relaxed and stress free.

Let's start with the equipment you will need to begin your knitting lesson. Don't be afraid, it will not cut deeply into your pocket money as you only need a handful of equipment to start your journey- yarn, knitting needles, a crochet hook, small scissors and, as a final touch, a container to store your supplies in. I know you are ready to rush out the store to get your supplies right now, but hold on, there is a twist here.

Knitting may be the only hobby that does not require much equipment. These tools are not costly and are also easily available. As a beginner, you are surely excited to start knitting you first project, but you need to prepare yourself with all of your knitting tools before starting the journey. Now it's time for shopping. Yes, you will finally get to enter those stores, filled with different types of knitting needles and colorful yarns, that you have always wanted to visit but were clueless about what pick. In this chapter you will learn about all of the equipment required for knitting, and how to pick the best of each.

Most knitters rush to the store in overexcitement and find themselves puzzled, spending a lot of money on unnecessary items like several pairs of knitting needles (which remain mostly untouched), various types of yarn and things they may never even need. My suggestion would be to take a little bit of time to choose the items you need before actually going shopping, which will help save your time and money.

Firstly, special care should be taken before selecting a pair of knitting needles. Now, what are knitting needles? Why should I buy them when I have my chopsticks around? Don't they look identical? The answer is no. You could try to start with it, but I can assure you that you will end up biting your nails in aggravation. When the beginning does not click, the chances of successful accomplishment of the mission can be affected.

Needle size is measured depending on the diameter of the needle. In the US the needle is given a simple number, but in Europe it is measured in millimeters. Different sizes are available for knitters to choose from, as different projects require different gauge needles. Though it's completely up to the knitter what size to pick, it is recommended that beginners pick one gauged between 10 and 14; this size needle is easy to handle and has less chance of slipping a stitch while knitting. Don't be afraid at the mention of the term "slipping a stitch", we will discuss the matter within our next segments.

Needles are not only different sizes, but are made of different materials as well. Several materials are used to make needles such as metals, plastics, bamboo and even wood. The material a needle is made of may not affect the experts in delivering their masterpiece, but for the novice, picking the right one is very important. Beginning with a pair of bamboo or wooden needles is always recommended for the new knitter, as they are a bit rougher in texture and reduce the chance of slipping stitches. On the other hand, plastic and metal needles are more slippery, which is why they are more difficult for beginners to use when getting started with this new skill. If you are looking for a cheaper alternative to bamboo or wood needles go for the plastic ones, as wood and bamboo needles are much more costly.

Now it's time to choose your yarn. No need to mention that there are ample options here as well, some yarns are very thin while others are thick and even super bulky. The presence of different materials can be seen here too, but natural fibers like wool, cotton, linen, or silk are much easier to handle. Yarn should be selected by keeping in mind the category of the project, whether you are making a scarf, gloves, blanket, or something else. Though I do not suggest that you spend $20 to $30 dollars for your first skein of yarn, I will also suggest that you not go with the cheapest option, either. After all, this is your first attempt and you don't want to end up with a mess. Poor quality of the cheaper yarns may frustrate you; usually these are too thick to handle well and may even break in the middle of a project. Preferably, choose the yarn that is in your budget range and that you find most comfortable to work with. If you are a new knitter, my advice is to pick a light colored yarn, as it reduces the chance of missing stitches as you would with a darker color. You could also choose your favorite color to boost your enthusiasm, but stay away from choosing multicolored yarn for your beginning knitting lessons.